BOOK OF ONIAS

BOOK OF ONIAS

by

R. C. CROSSFIELD

PHILOSOPHICAL LIBRARY
New York

When, therefore, any man, no matter who, or how high his standing may be, utters or publishes anything which afterwards proves to be untrue, he is a false prophet. And if he does it un- called for, for the purpose of injuring his fellow beings, *or for the sake of gain,* or to deceive any man by putting a false coloring upon a matter of religion, to lead astray or prejudice the minds of any to hinder them from receiving the truth, woe unto him, for he is a false prophet! — Here then we can say, where we find a person uttering or publishing what he does not know to be a truth, merely to make a noise, whereby the least saint on earth might be offended (he is a false prophet)— beware of false prophets.

Printed in the *Evening and Morning Star,* July, 1833.

Foreword

The Word of God, given to the Prophet Onias comprising Sections 1 to 22 of the Book of Onias, received at various intervals from March 1961 to this date. (Also a Revelation on the Nature of God and the creation.)

This material is not authorized by the Trustee in Trust of the Church of Jesus Christ of Latter Day Saints and should be read only as non-authorized scripture. Discretion should be used in placing this in the hands of the ignorant and those who would use it to discredit the Church.

It is not the purpose of the author, in presenting this to the Church membership, to ridicule or criticize the Church but to present the revelations for their judgment. These revelations should in no way be construed as encouraging dissension or apostasy from the Church, for these revelations prove beyond a doubt that the Church is the only Church recognized by God on the earth today.

These revelations should be an inspiration to those who read them to live closer to God and keep his commandments more perfectly.

Introduction

Revelation received March 30, 1965

Behold, I say unto you all, ye nations of the earth, yea, all who come within the sound of My Voice, for I perceive the thoughts and intents of all men, and they are surely known unto Me, for there is no prayer that is not considered nor is there a curse that is hidden. To these all, I say unto you repent, for the Kingdom of Heaven is nigh at hand. To those who are members of My Church and particularly the leaders of My Church I also say unto you repent, for you now ignore and have ignored My servants whom I have sent. You ignore the wailings of the widows and orphans who pray continually upon Me for deliverance, and you place upon them burdens that ye yourself would not be willing to bear, and then condemn them for their actions if they do err. Behold, I say unto you that their sins shall be counted upon your heads, and when ye stand before Me, ye shall have no excuse, for My Gospel is plainly written so that even a child can therein understand. But by some device of mind ye excuse yourselves, saying that such things are done away with. Behold I say unto you I detract none of My law and to those who know and understand and live not, they are under condemnation, and shall be made to answer before My judgment at that day appointed. Behold, have I not said concerning those whose spouses have committed adultery and who have been true and faithful, that they shall be given to him that hath not committed adultery, but hath been faithful, for thus it is decreed that the faithful be made

1

ruler over many. Behold, I say unto you, — do ye do this? I say unto you nay, and many other things ye do not, that I have commanded, supposing that they are not now necessary. But I say unto you that this is My law so that the innocent may not suffer, for a man by nature will take care of his own, but hesitates to take care of that which to him does not belong. Yea, ye use as your excuse that the law of the land forbids this. Behold, I say unto you, it is not the law that ye fear, but the persecution that follows those that keep all My commandments. Behold, My servant Joseph Smith, which ye do now claim as a prophet, and do honor him in his rightful place. Behold, I say unto you that he feared not men and continually petitioned the unrighteous judge to seek justice and redress for the wrongs done to My people and to those he loved. And now I command that ye shall continually seek the rectification of the law of this land to the end that My saints can keep all My commandments according to the law, and if they hear not thy petition and allow them not to keep My commandments and ye do all in your power to bring this about, then I shall fight your battles and then shall this rebellious nation be destroyed as My will shall decree.

But if ye keep not My commandments and seek not to bring about My will concerning this nation, behold, it is because ye fear men, and esteem the world of greater worth than My Kingdom, and to be carnally minded is death, for thus it is to be carnally minded.

Behold, My servant whom I have sent is but dung, and for this reason ye esteem him not, but for this reason I use those that are weak and not learned in the ways of men, for if a man come in his wisdom, ye shall say it is of man, for by his wisdom he doth obtain this knowledge. But if I send one who is not learned, behold, ye cannot say by his own wisdom he doeth this thing, then is it not of God? Behold, I do send My servant, and in him I do place My Spirit and by his weaknesses he is made

2

strong, for without them I cannot convince My people.

Where do ye stand then, My friends? For ye still remain My friends until ye openly rebel against Me, for now is the time to repent and thy sins shall be forgiven thee, and by My Spirit shall the truth of these things be made manifest, and by this Spirit, if ye remain faithful, ye shall know the truth of all things. Dwell not upon the things of this earth, but upon heavenly things that thy soul may be lifted up unto the understanding of a higher knowledge. Be not despondent but encouraged. Fight for that which ye know to be right and be not afraid. Courage, onward to a victory that shall culminate in lives everlasting to your eternal glory for evermore. Let thy minds be pure so that My Spirit may dwell within thee, and let thy hands be clean and free from the shedding of innocent blood, for this is an unpardonable sin which resulted in My servant David in losing his portion of My Kingdom. Be as serpents wise and as doves innocent. Be perfect in all things and heed the counsel of My servants. Even so amen.

Section 1

Revelation received February or March 1961

Thus saith the Lord God: — Not until the Church again
lives the new and everlasting covenant as revealed to them in
plainness by My servant the prophet Joseph Smith and verified
from time to time by others of My holy prophets, will I instruct
and guide this Church with further enlightenment. For if ye
will not receive the word ye have, what profit will it be if I
reveal more to you? For you will treat it as naught and trample
it under your feet.

Repent, therefore, both the sheep and the shepherd and I will
reveal more of the mysteries of My Kingdom, for I will give
here a little and there a little, line upon line and precept upon
precept, if ye will have it, until you have all truth and are able
to stand in My presence. For My Word is as a refiner's fire,
dividing the evil from the good, and sharper than a two-edged
sword dividing asunder both bone and marrow.

Repent therefore! Come unto Me, all ye that are heavy laden
and I will give you rest. Call upon My name both day and
night and repent of your many iniquities and I will forgive
you, and you will again be acceptable as My Church. For there
are many among you, even of your leaders and those who
call themselves your leaders who are not acceptable in My
sight, for they do corrupt the right ways of the Lord and do
pervert My doctrines which I have so plainly revealed to you
in the Book of Mormon and the Doctrine and Covenants. This
they do because they have not the spirit and seek after the

5

glory of the world and not My Glory, for I see their works, and know their acts, and they are not of Me, and I have not sent them.

Repent therefore, and come unto Me and learn of My ways and I will be your shepherd and ye will be My sheep. Amen.

And again that same afternoon, shortly after.

Thus saith the Lord: — Woe unto them that seek to hide their counsel from the Lord, who pervert the ways of the Lord and by their many words flatter many away on forbidden paths saying that sin is not sin. To turn away the widows and orphans, — I say unto you is this not sin? Ye know that it is, but you excuse yourselves saying, "We are busy doing the Lord's work." I say unto you, is this not the Lord's work, to feed the widows and the orphans? Woe unto the Bishops of My Church who deny the poor, for they shall be accountable before Me when they stand before My Judgment and unless they speedily repent they shall be cast off.

Marvel not how these revelations come, for My ways are strange ways and not after the understanding of men, and I use the small and contemptible things of the world to bring to pass My marvelous works, for they shall be brought forth even in spite of the wicked. I have sent My servant Onias for this purpose, for is he not contemptible and is esteemed as naught among his brethren? Ask Me if these things are not of Me? Have I not said, seek and ye shall find, knock and it shall be opened unto you? But I say unto you, there are many who seek after a sign, but signs shall follow those that believe and ye shall know them by their works. Amen.

Section 2

Revelation received May 9th, 1961

Thus saith the Lord: — Behold, the time is now ripe and nigh at hand when the land of Missouri will be reclaimed from the wicked and be given to My Saints. Yea, those who are pure in heart shall have an inheritance therein.

Let those who have much wealth impart unto the Church their monies to purchase an inheritance in Zion and let those who have much wealth impart it unto the poor so that they may also obtain equal inheritance in Zion, for thus it behooveth Me. This I lay as a commandment and woe unto those who covet their wealth and will not impart it unto the poor, for their inheritance will be taken from them.

When properties are put up for sale by the inhabitants of Independence and the surrounding countries, let chosen elders, ones who are trustworthy, purchase these properties, and by this means the lands of their inheritance, even Zion, shall gradually be reclaimed from the wicked. This must be done according to the commandments I have given you, even in My Book, the Doctrine and Covenants; obeying the laws of the land in all things pertaining to this matter.

Let not those who are wicked know of these matters lest Satan take hold of their hearts and make a stumbling block for My Saints.

All those who pay a full tithe whether rich or poor, and who keep all My commandments are worthy to have an inheritance

7

in Zion, and this is how they shall be chosen. However widows and those destitute and who are living My commandments are exempt, and may receive an inheritance. Even so Amen.

Woe unto them that mock My servant Onias, for they shall be naught. I know his faults and they are many, however, I do not use the wise things of the world to bring to pass My marvelous works but use the small and contemptible things, yea, even those things that men despise and esteem as naught.

Let My servant move as seemeth him good, for I have not called him to any other calling except to receive My oracles. Therefore let his mind be at peace. Nevertheless let him beware of his weaknesses lest Satan tempt him and he be overcome.

Do not at this time send this revelation to My servant the President of My Church, even David O. McKay, for he pondereth these things you have sent him in his mind and I say this unto you, so you may have a witness that I know his thoughts and doings, and this is the witness ye have asked of Me. Therefore be content for the present. Even so Amen.

Section 3

Revelation received July 16th, 1961

There is a way that man may speak to God and if he is worthy he shall receive it.

Also the following the same day.

Thus saith the Lord: — Ye have not chosen Me but I have chosen thee to be a prophet unto this people, therefore why murmur thee and concern yourself over this matter. Know ye not that I choose the contemptible things of this earth, yea, even those things that the world despiseth, nevertheless thou has sinned, and unless thou speedily repenteth, Satan desireth thy soul, for he delighteth in the sins of men and rejoiceth in their iniquities. Humble thyself, and seek not to exalt thyself above others, and I shall make thee strong, yea, even I will place My Spirit in thee, that thou may reveal greater things unto this people, yea, even the hidden things I have kept hidden from the foundation of the world, yea, even until this time. Yea, I showed them unto others of My holy prophets, yea, even did I show them unto Joseph Smith, but the world was not yet ready to receive them so I commanded him to restrain himself that he would not reveal it unto the people at that time, for they were not yet ready to receive these things, for they would have been a stumbling block to them, yea, even they would have fallen because of them, for their minds were not yet prepared, neither were they wholly cleansed from the darkness that covered their eyes.

9

Hear ye O My people of My Church. Know ye not that I am God and I reveal all My truths in My own due time. Know ye not that I have power to summon the seas, and mountains shall come from their midst? Know ye not that I have power to summon the great mountains and they shall become the bottom of the ocean? Know ye not that I shall gather mine elect from the four quarters of the earth, yea, and they shall assemble themselves in Zion, and a great shout of joy shall go forth unto the ends of the earth, yea, and all shall hear the shout and know that I am Lord, yea, even thy God, yea, and none shall stay their hand, and they shall be as a devouring fire, yea, even as stubble is burned by fire so shall they devour the wicked by fire.

Yea, and there shall go a decree forth out of Heaven that every knee shall bow and every tongue shall confess that Jesus is the Lord, the Savior of the world, yea, even Jehovah the Mighty one of Israel, who shall come out of Heaven to the inhabitants of the earth, to reign a thousand years. Yea, I say unto you, even Jesus Christ your Redeemer, that the time is nigh at hand, even at the door, for all things to be fulfilled. Yea, I have trodden the winepress alone and now My wrath is full, yea, even will I pour out My vengeance upon the wicked for they are nigh ripened in iniquity, yea, they do all kinds of abominations and wickedness, and their hearts are so hard that My Word has no place in them. Nevertheless, there are many among them who yet can be brought into My fold. Therefore thrust in your sickle with all your might, yea, even from early in the morning until your laying down at night and ye shall not lose your reward.

However many of you are not prepared, for you are as the foolish virgins, for they had no fuel for their lamps and were left when the bridegroom came. Therefore repent, even now, and humble thyself even to the earth. Seek after knowledge and wisdom, for you have dissipated away your talents and now there is but little time left. The harvest is now ripe, yea, even the kernels do fall from the ear, yea, and many do join the Church of their own free will having no elders to teach them.

The harvest is great but the laborers are few. Yea, many are called but few are chosen. Why are they not chosen? Because they dissipate away their time and do not study diligently My Gospel. Yea, their minds are filled with the cares of this world, and they say, "let me first go and bury my father." Yea, for their father is the world, and unless ye leave this world ye have no part of Me.

O Father, that I may shout thy praise above the stars, and shout praises to Thee forever. Yea, for thou hast again restored thy Gospel and brought forth again thy Word. O that I could shout with the voice of Gabriel, for he did shout and the walls of Heaven shook.

Hear ye, hear ye, all ye nations of the earth, repent, for the Kingdom of Heaven is at hand. A prophet, O ye people, has restored the gospel, yea, even in its fullness, yea, and angels have spoken from Cumorah. The Priesthood has been restored, bringing with it the New and Everlasting covenant that we on earth may again enter into God's presence.

Hear all ye nations of the earth; for the Lord reigneth and He only is our God. Amen.

11

Section 4

Revelation received Aug. 27, 1961

Show not these revelations unto the wicked, for they shall destroy thee. These revelations are given to the righteous only, for their benefit that they may learn doctrine and become more perfect before Me.

Section 5

Revelation received Sept. 16, 1961

Thus saith the Lord: — As I have commanded before, I will command again, that unless the people of My Church live the new and everlasting covenant of marriage as I have commanded them in My Book, the Doctrine and Covenants, even in its fullness, they can not enter into the land of their inheritance, even Independence, Missouri and the regions round about. This I have commanded many times, but ye have not yet repented of this sin which ye have committed, and ye have been damned even that your eternal progress has been stopped. And for this reason I have not given unto you further revelation, for ye were not able to stand that even which ye had. For I am a just God and I give here a little and there a little, line upon line, precept upon precept, until ye have all My words and are able to stand in My presence. Nevertheless it was expedient for a time that ye should refrain from entering into this covenant that the Church be not overthrown by its enemies.

Yea, but now mine enemies and also your enemies shall have no more power over thee, for they shall be confused and their arms shall be raised in contention with their brethren, even that they will contend one with another unto their final destruction.

Ye shall not move forward any faster then ye are able, and all things shall be done in order even as I have commanded.

For there have been many false prophets in My Church who have heaped upon this people many false doctrines, yea, but their false prophecies shall be made known and they shall be confounded and be cast out, yea, for they secretly sought to bring destruction to My Church and they did teach these things that they might be lifted up in the eyes of men, yea, for they did esteem the glory of men rather then the Glory of God. And they shall be cast out and not enter into My rest which I have preserved for the righteous.

Neither shall those who withhold their tithe enter into My rest, for they have not sufficient faith, and their faith is evidenced by their work, and their works are not pleasing in My sight, therefore they shall be cast off at the last day if they do not speedily repent.

Neither shall those who do not keep all My commandments enter into My rest, for there are many in the Church who are lifted up in the pride of their hearts, and do esteem themselves greater than their brethren, even to oppressing them in little matters. And there are many in My Church who seek after offices, even that they would fain buy their offices with flattery and great speaking. And I will reveal these unto you that they may be cast out, for ye shall not spare nor fear what man can do, for if ye live My commandments and have My Spirit, ye cannot be confounded, neither can ye be killed or slain.

Now I speak unto those that call themselves the leaders of My Church, for ye have not altogether heeded My words that I have given you, even that ye have set aside the words I have given through My servant Onias, and ye have esteemed them as naught. Also ye have feared them lest they be true, and ye have not followed My instruction in that I said; "seek and ye shall find, knock and it shall be opened unto you." Yea, and unless ye heed these words ye shall be cast off, for I have chosen already others to take your place, yea, for at My Word

16

I can raise up of these stones, seed unto Abraham, your father, who is My faithful servant, for he shall not lose the promise which I have made to him in that through his seed all kingdoms of the earth shall be blessed.

For if ye heed not the words which I have given I will withdraw My Spirit from among you and ye shall have no power and ye shall be as other men, yea, ye shall stumble in your words and your tongue shall cleave to the roof of your mouth, and your words shall be as babbling, and then shall ye know that I am God, and unless ye speedily repent ye shall be cast off even as I have before promised. For ye shall be as the Pharisees and hypocrites, yea, for they cast out the prophets and stoned them to death.

Yea, but I am well pleased with My servant Hugh B. Brown, for I know his thoughts and the intents of his heart and they are pure before Me and he shall be a shaft in My hand, yea, even a polished shaft to the confounding of the wicked, yea, and I command him that he will refrain from that which hath been given him, for not at any time have I commanded that there shall be more than three in the Presidency of My Church, for this is confusion unto Me. I know also the thoughts and intents of My servant Mark E. Peterson, for he is a choice spirit unto Me and I am well pleased with him, and he has repented of the pride which was in his heart, for which I am well pleased, for he has prayed much unto Me concerning these matters, and My Spirit has spoken oft to him, yea, he shall not lose his reward. Yea, and many others there be in the Presidency of My Church who are faithful, and do diligently seek after the truth, and look forward faithfully to that which is to come.

But I am not well pleased with My servant Henry D. Moyle, for he is lifted up in the pride of his heart and his thoughts are not altogether right before Me, for he doteth upon his riches, yea, and his heart is set upon them, yea, for is it not

17

harder for a rich man to enter into My Kingdom than for a camel to go through the eye of a needle? Nevertheless if he gives all he has to the poor, then can he be saved.

Yea, I am not well pleased with My servant David O. McKay, even the president of My Church, for he has done things which I have not commanded and hath feared men. Nevertheless he shall soon be in My presence to account for his deeds.

I say unto all nations, yea, and even all those who call themselves after My name, to repent, for the Kingdom of Heaven is at hand, and the time soon cometh when the Son of Man, even your Savior Jesus Christ, doth come to reign as King of Kings and Lord of Lords, yea, and woe unto them who are unable to withstand His coming, for they shall be as stubble.

I say unto My servant Onias that he repent of all his sins, for no sin is acceptable in My sight, and all evil is an abomination to Me; nevertheless his righteous desires are acceptable before Me and they shall all be fulfilled in mine own due time.

Section 6

Revelation received Nov. 19, 1961

Show not these things I have revealed unto thee to My servant (Radomach) for he is rebellious and has not kept all My commandments. Nevertheless, because of his many grievous afflictions I have supported him.

Be patient, for thou art lacking in this matter. I do all things in mine own due time and it is not necessary for thee to show these things unto any others than thou hast, for these things shall be given to the world in mine own due time.

Section 7

Revelation received Dec. 1961

Fear not, for I am with thee, for all that I have told thee will surely come to pass, for those things I have not told thee that are not My Word, shall not come to pass, for thou hast sinned in that thou has assumed things that I have not said, therefore repent and write only those things that I command, otherwise thou shall be destroyed. Satan tempteth thee and seeketh thy soul. Beware lest ye be overcome. My vengeance is about to be poured out upon all nations, yea, even some of the destruction I have promised is about to be poured out upon the earth without measure.

Section 8

Revelation received Jan. 24, 1962

The question you asked was this. "What is meant by the scripture, even chapter 6 of Moroni and verse #1?" When I showed Myself at that time to the Nephites after My resurrection there was no true organization existing on the earth resembling My Church, for there was such great wickedness upon the face of the earth before My coming that the Church set up by My servant Alma was taken from among men. However, there were many of those not destroyed at that time who still held the Priesthood and had not sinned sufficiently to have their Priesthood taken from them. For this reason they were not destroyed and survived the great desolation which destruction came at the time of My death at Jerusalem. These men, therefore, to enter into My Kingdom, which is the Church of Jesus Christ, had to be baptized, and had to show forth fruit meet for repentance in that they had repented of their unbelief. And when they had done this they were baptized and received the Holy Ghost. However, they did not again have to be ordained to the Priesthood, for they had already been given this.

Whenever there has been sufficient righteousness upon the earth I have tried to establish My Church among the children of men, but oft they have not understood, and My Church has been taken from among them but My Priesthood has remained, and My servants, who I have chosen, even the prophets,

23

have exhorted the people to repentance, and when the people have rejected even their prophesying, even the Priesthood has been taken from among men, and then falleth destruction, yea, even the total destruction which fell upon the Nephites, for they willingly rebelled against Me and were conscious of the evil they were committing, even unto their condemnation, for My Spirit will not always strive with the children of men, for My Spirit can act only when men are willing. Nevertheless I chastise those whom I love that they may be brought down unto the depths of humility, whereby they may come before Me with a broken heart and a contrite spirit and know the true love of God. But when men's hearts become so hard that they reject My Word, even when they are chastised, they are beyond feeling, and My Spirit can no longer strive with them, and then they are nigh ripe for destruction.

For whoso heareth My Word and live it, blessed is he, for his light shall shine before men that they may see it and glorify God. And then shall much good be done among the children of men and many souls saved from an awful hell.

Repent therefore all ye ends of the earth that ye may be spared at the last day, for that day speedily cometh, and the signs and wonders which I have promised have already begun to come to pass, and the third of the host of Heaven, yea, even those who were cast out, even Satan and his angels, and those who chose compulsion, are raging in the hearts of men, yea, even taking possession of their bodies, causing them to commit all types of heinous crimes and sins, for they know that their time is short, and that they have but little time left, for they shall be cast into outer darkness that they may no longer be able to tempt men, yea, even for a thousand years. Then they shall be let loose for a short season to gather their armies and then shall the end come.

Show these things not unto the wicked for they are like swine and will trample these pearls under their feet and turn and rend thee. Nevertheless send the things that thou has chosen to the person called Hope for in the past she hast done much good but now has become surrounded in sin, and has accepted as truth that which is evil, and has not asked Me if these things be true, for she hath been led astray by that evil one who seeks to destroy all My works and bring confusion and strife among My people. For he seeks to destroy the things of God, yea, he lays in wait and catches the unwary and those who are weak in the Church, for he delighteth in sin and his joy is in confusion. Nevertheless thou hast grieved the Spirit in this thing, for ye seek to become great in the eyes of men. Repent of this wickedness lest thou be destroyed. Humble yourself before Me that I may reveal many great and marvelous things that have beforehand not come unto the children of men because of their wickedness, and their wickedness is that of unbelief, and they live not the commandments that I place before them, and do trample them under their feet and esteem them not. Oh how oft I would have gathered ye as a hen gathereth her chicks under her wing but ye would not. Ye are a stiffnecked people, and have been from the beginning, and have not diligently sought Me in all matters, but have gone on in your own wisdom ignoring the instructions that have been given thee to your own condemnation. For have I not instructed thee to ask and it shall be opened unto thee, seek and ye shall find. Seek after wisdom and knowledge, for they are most precious gifts. Seek not for that which doth cancer the soul, for it rendeth and breaketh into pieces and hence it is good for nothing, and must be cast aside and be as dung.

Harken O ye servants of the Lord, even the Presidency of My Church, for ye have a responsibility laid upon you to all of the saints who have accepted My Gospel and do diligently seek to keep My commandments.

25

Section 9

Revelation received March 7 and 11, 1962

Harken O ye elders of My Church and listen to Him who is above you all; and knoweth all their desires and intents, for they are all laid before Me by the power of My Spirit.*

Yea, even harken to the voice of your Redeemer and Savior Jesus Christ. For all the things that I have decreed will be made manifest and shall surely come to pass, for My Word is as a refiner's fire, separating the good from the evil, and sharper than a two-edged sword dividing asunder both bone and marrow.

Repent, I say unto you repent, for the Kingdom of Heaven is nigh at hand, yea, even at the doors. Take, therefore, My laws for your protection, for houses of stone, nor armor or towers or pits will protect the wicked from My Judgment.

For neighbour shall take up sword against neighbour, and they shall fall upon each other in anger, and town shall be against town, and city against city, and state against state, and country against country, and the righteous must needs flee to Zion and to those places appointed.

Harken O ye elders of My Church, yea, even the presiding High Council of My Church, yea, and even they who call themselves the First Presidency. Gird up your loins round about yourselves and seek counsel from Me. Beware lest ye stumble and fall and others take your place, for ye are nigh ready for destruction, for ye seek My voice in the High Places and thy

---

*Added April 1, 1962.

words come back to thee as brass. Beware, even the President of My Church, even David O. McKay, for he pretendeth revelation, for he doth know and I your Savior know he receiveth no revelation. He receiveth inspiration to guide My Church and this for the sake of the righteous, for My House will not be left desolate, for I will raise up one mighty and strong among you, having the sceptre of justice in his hand, who shall grind in pieces all those who would oppose My work, for the prayer of the righteous shall not go unheeded.

Yea, I have commanded and My commandments have gone unheeded, and the pattern is being followed of those in olden days who heeded not the prophet's warning, and were destroyed, for great wickedness reigneth in the city that is called Salt Lake and all the cities and communities round about. Nevertheless there are many who are pure in heart among them, and many do please Me greatly for their righteous acts and thoughts. They do send up a sweet savor to the Lord of Saboth, which interpreted means Creator of the First Day.

And thus I command My servants, the Presidency of My Church, that they repent of their unbelief and humble themselves before Me and keep My commandments. For I command them that they shall appoint a committee, yea, even as seemeth them good; wise men and just, and seek redress through the laws of this country to reclaim the lands of Zion from the wicked. For much of this land was purchased by the saints at the time of My servant even Joseph Smith and they were driven contrary to the laws of the land even from their inheritance, yea, even search all the old records and deeds, and place them before the courts of this country, and My Spirit will be with them, that they may lay bare the wrongs done to My servants that all may see. Then if the judges and those that are placed in authority, even your rulers, do not admit these wrongs and restore the lands and properties that rightfully belong to My saints, then I will utterly destroy them

28

from off the face of the earth that they no longer stand in the path of righteousness. I command also that another committee be set up of wise and just men, even as seemeth ye good, to search out again the records, notes and proceedings, against the Church concerning the Temple Lot Suit, in the which the property dedicated by My servants, even at the time of the Prophet Joseph Smith, was given into the hands of an apostate group, even the ground of the Temple which shall be established in this generation if ye shall keep all My commandments. And ye shall not fear men or what they can do but ye shall fear God, for the sons of men put heavy burdens upon your shoulders grievous to be borne, but My yoke is easy and leadeth to peaceful pastures, yea, even eternal lives.

And ye shall lay bare before the leaders of this country the wrongs done in this matter, and if they admit not these wrongs, and restore not unto My saints their rightful inheritance, I shall destroy them from off the face of the earth.

And this I lay as a commandment that ye do these things and seek no more the glory of the world but My Glory, otherwise ye have no promise and your inheritance shall be given unto others, for My Word shall not be mocked.

And if the leaders of this nation restore not unto you these properties, and ye do all in your power laying the facts before the courts of this land, then I shall utterly destroy this nation, for it puffeth itself up in the eyes of all the world saying "Who is like unto the United States? Behold, her mighty munitions, behold her chariots and towers and many great and spacious buildings." Behold, I say unto you, unless she repenteth of her wickedness she shall be destroyed, and her great cities wherewith she boasteth of shall become heaps of rubble, and all her tall towers wherewith she boasteth of shall become heaps and none shall be able to dwell therein, and I shall send famine and pestilence among her like as she has never heard, and then shall they know that I am the Lord, and reward every man according as his works shall be. Even so, Amen.

Section 10

Revelation received April 7, 1962

This I lay as a commandment: — Prepare yourself to move, let your affairs be in order, pay your debts, and if it so be that thou art worthy, for thou hast sinned in a grievous manner before Me, it shall be given unto thee that thou will be made great among thy brethren. However, repent of this thing in sackcloth and ashes that thou may be pure before Me to receive My oracles as they shall be given unto you. Teach not if ye have not the Holy Ghost, for without this utterance thou art as dross. Be patient in all things and exercise thy faith in all that thou doest that thy light shall shine before men that they may see your good works and glorify your Father who is in Heaven. Be diligent in all that thou doest that thou may not be counted a sluggard. Attend to thy duties both at home and in Church that all thy works may be perfect before Me. Prepare thyself for offices in the Church that will call upon all thy resources. Pray always that thou will not be led into temptation and faint. Gird up thy loins about thee and be ever prepared for that which is to come. Trouble yourself not about Mammon, for thou shalt have sufficient for thy needs. Teach thy children the peaceable things of the Kingdom, for they are choice spirits having the seed of Israel. Thou art a chosen vessel unto Me and if thou wilt have it, thou will do many things to prepare this people for My coming. Be content for the present and keep the commandments as I have commanded thee.

Section 11

Revelation received July 30, 1962

Ye have not kept My commandments wherein I commanded you to show these things to none other than to those you had already shown them to, and because of this ye had lost your gift for a time. For all things I command, I command for a purpose, and if men do not what I say they have no promise, and this I do to try men to see if they are worthy to receive the gifts that I will bestow upon them.

Ye have asked Me several times if the revelations ye have received from Me are true. When My Spirit came upon you this night and you prayed immediately to Me and asked Me if the Spirit was true, and when you prayed in this manner "O Father in Heaven, even the Father of my spirit, I beseech thee in the name of thy Son Jesus Christ, and ask thee if this spirit which I have received is true, and if it is thy Spirit, I ask thee in the name of thy Son Jesus Christ that it may tarry with me, and if it be not of thee, O God the Eternal Father, I command in the name of thy Son Jesus Christ that it depart far from me."

And in this manner ye have asked Me and ye know that the Spirit hath remained with thee, and it is contrary to the order of Heaven to lie, therefore ye have tried the spirits and ye know from which source they came. Therefore ye know of a surety that these things are true and so shall ye know the truth of all things if ye will be faithful to keep all My commandments.

Fear not to keep My commandments. Fear not men for they can afflict you in body, but fear rather that which can rob thee of thy spirit, for Satan desireth it mightily and seeks to entangle thee in his snare to secure ye fast and bind you with the fetters of sin and claim you his own.

O beware, O beware, of the power of Satan, for a gaping, yawning pit awaiteth those that serve him, a pit of anguish and an awful looking forward to the judgments of God and a perfect knowledge of one's guilt, wherein there is weeping and wailing and gnashing of teeth. And this I have shown to some but immediately closed the scene from their vision lest they be consumed with sorrow.

O that men may see the error of their ways and be converted and turn to Me, their Savior, with full purpose of heart that they may dwell with Me in the presence of the Father forever. Even so, Amen.

Section 12

Revelation received Sept. 27, 1962

Behold I say unto you at this time. Be of good cheer for those whom I call I chastise and try, lest when the battle is at its height they fall. Ye have been tried, and yet will be tried, for I prove all who would come unto Me. Behold and give ear and strive diligently to keep the commandments as I have given you. Strive to pay thy debts that thou hast accumulated against My instructions, and if thou wilt strive with all thy might thou wilt be blessed to this end. Pray always and faint not. Murmur not at thy afflictions for they teach thee wisdom.

Know ye not that when ye serve Me the whole world is against you, for the world lieth in sin and even those of thy brethren shall revile against thee and there will be those who shall even seek thy life. Study those things that ye have been given and be not negligent in thy duties. This is all for the present.

Section 13

Revelation received August 12, 1962

Ye have asked Me what ye should do with the revelations ye have received. Behold, I say unto you, inasmuch as ye have prepared them in the manner ye have, I now command you: Place them in a safe place until ye receive further instructions from Me. Do not at any time place these in the hands of the wicked, for they shall turn and rend thee and cause thee much affliction. Again thou art tempted to become great in the eyes of thy brethren and because ye have heeded Satan in his temptings in the past it has caused you much affliction of soul. Do therefore what I command and heed not men, so that I may use thee as My servant, and that thou may be instructed more perfectly in doctrine, otherwise thou shalt be cast off and another take thy place.

Behold, I say unto you that there is but one appointed at this time to receive revelation from Me and this I do that confusion reigneth not. But I appoint many as prophets who testify of the truth of these things, for the testimony of Jesus Christ is the spirit of prophecy, for whoso hath a testimony of Me hath received of My Spirit and knoweth of a surety that these things are true. Therefore thou art chosen. Prepare thyself by study and prayer, calling upon the name of God continually that thou will not be overcome.

Section 14

Revelation received Jan. 17, 1963

Behold, I say unto you at this time, prepare the works ye have received at My hand, even the revelations thou hast received at diverse times. Prepare them for printing even by study and diligence, and by inspiration that it may be an acceptable work unto Me, and thou shalt do the work thyself, by thine own hand, and ways and means shall be provided that thou mayest be able to accomplish this work if thou do it with all diligence.

Yea, and there are many things that thou desireth to know which ye shall surely obtain knowledge of if thou art diligent, but because of thy weaknesses I am constrained, and I cannot reveal these things unto you at this time lest thou fall and be overcome. Prove thyself in all things and be not despondent, for I am with thee and surely watching over thee, that thou be not destroyed before thou hast accomplished the things I commanded and will require of thee if thou art diligent.

Behold, I say unto thee, thou art desirous of another wife which thing is pleasing in My sight, but thy garments are not yet fully clean and on occasion thou dost list to the temptings of Satan. Prepare thyself more fully for this, for this is in fulfillment of the commandments I have given to the children of men, which if they keep in holiness their reward shall be great.

Behold, I say unto you, because My Church has not lived this commandment and have feared men rather then their God, behold, I say unto you, they have been damned, even that I have given unto them no further enlightenment, for they trample that which they have under their feet, esteeming the wisdom of men as more worth than the wisdom of their God, saying boldly that God no longer requires this of them, for they seek the praise of the world, and are ashamed of the Holy covenants of God. And it was because of their fear and much complaining that the fullness of the Gospel, even the New and Everlasting covenant in its fullness was taken from among them. Therefore, I command the leaders of My Church to excercise the authority they have in them, even the authority I gave to the Prophet Joseph Smith, yea, even the sealing powers, to bind on earth as in Heaven, even in their fullness.

Even then shall I again speak to them face to face and My curse shall be taken from them for by My Word I am bound.

But behold, I say unto thee, that if ye reject this commandment which I have given through My servant Onias then shall they know My vengeance saith the Lord. For My house shall be clean and even by the power of My Word I shall do it, even all that I have spoken of this matter. Even so, Amen.

Behold, I say unto you, prepare thyself to move and seek suitable employment in the United States and I will bless you in this matter even that thou will be able to provide for thy family. Prepare thyself for important things to come. Write again to that person called Hope, for she has begun to repent of the evil she has committed and even, if she will have it, she will help thee in the preparation of this material even for its printing. Write unto her even as I shall dictate and this I lay as a commandment, even so, Amen.

Section 15

Revelation received March, 1963

Thy sins are forgiven thee if thou truly repent and prepare these things as I have asked. Seek not for positions in My Church as the wicked do, so they may be seen of man, but let thy influence be felt for good wherever you are and whatever your task may be so that you may bring many into My Church. For this is your calling, that you may call repentance unto this nation and cause many to repent of their sins and turn again unto Me. This is all for the present, Amen.

Section 16

Revelation received March 31, 1963

Behold, I say unto you. As ye have prepared this work for printing and ye have prepared it even in your weakness. This I say unto you. Send all three copies that thou hast typewritten to My servant even Joseph Fielding Smith, even the president of the Presiding High Council, even the Quorum of the Twelve Apostles. This is a commandment that I give unto you which, if ye do, ye shall be blessed.

Behold, I say unto you, I will do unto Hope as seemeth Me good as she has not done as I commanded her, and has returned to her gods which are the gods of mystery and confusion.

I say unto you, instruct My servant even Joseph Fielding Smith that he shall gather the other eleven that have been chosen as mine apostles that they study these things that thou has written and that they should call upon Me in united prayer and ask Me, their Savior, if these things are not of Me, and if they shall do this with sincere hearts having faith in Christ they shall know the truth of these things by the power of the Holy Ghost, for I shall manifest it unto them by this power and they shall test the spirits lest they be deceived.

And behold, I say unto thee, if they art faithful in doing this, an angel shall appear unto them as a witness that these things are true, and this angel shall be sent from My presence, and they shall test him as I have commanded in My Book, the Doctrine and Covenants. Howbeit he hath not a message until they have thoroughly repented of their sins. This I command and make known unto thee, even so, Amen.

Section 17

Revelation received August 25, 1963

Behold, I say unto you, now is the time that false Gods will abound in the earth and false prophets will be raised up in multitudes to deceive and confuse the people. Be not deceived, for I have not rejected My Church, but many of those who call themselves leaders of My Church I have already rejected, even that they no longer have their authority and have lost even what they had, through iniquity.

Behold, I command the leaders of My Church to repent of their sins, for they esteem the glory of the world of more worth than My Glory, and seek the praise of men for their good works rather than humble themselves before Me and seek My counsel. They praise not Me for their gifts and talents and riches but think that by their own works they have achieved these treasures. Behold, I say unto you that unless they repent they shall be less than dross, for their gifts shall be returned unto Him who gave them, their talents shall deteriorate, and their riches shall melt away, and then shall the dog return to his vomit, and the end shall be worse than the first, and their end from their beginning.

Behold, ye have My witness, ye have My law, ye have the means of determining right from wrong, ye have the Keys to determine truth from error, ye are left without excuse.

Section 18

Revelation received Nov. 23, 1964 and
thereafter as designated

Behold, I say unto you, even your Savior, saying with a loud voice, fear God and give glory to Him, for the time soon cometh when I shall come to govern My people, yea, even the Pure In Heart shall hear My voice and shall clap their hands with joy knowing their rest shall be glorious. Yea, even I give unto you a revelation, yea, even to the leaders of My Church, yea, even that they will cringe with fear and quake with fright, those that heed not My commandments, for the truth pierceth to the heart and maketh bare the wound and the wicked rage to hear it. Behold, I say unto you that ye covenant with Me that ye will keep the law as contained in the revelations received by My servant Joseph, even in the Book, the Doctrine and Covenants of My Church. Behold I say unto you, ye keep them not, and ye devise ways and means whereby ye excuse yourselves of these most sacred of covenants (Dec. 13, 1964) and ye seek continually to please the world, thinking only of the immediate rewards, but ye neglect the weightier matters which bring salvation to the soul and which bring rewards eternal. Repent even now, for ye shall not stand at the last day.

(Dec. 6, 1964) Behold, I say unto you, the leaders of My Church, that ye have distorted the truth of My Gospel and have changed and set up offices in My Church which are an abomination unto Me, and ye have appointed work and respon-

47

sibilities of some which belong to another, and ye have gone on in your own ways thinking that ye are wiser than God. Behold, I say unto you, listen and give ear and hear wisdom from your Savior and be not deceived. Behold, ye have set up offices in the Church called Assistants to the Quorum of Twelve Apostles. Behold, ye have received no commandment from Me to set up such an office, for such an office is not after the order of Heaven, which Church, if it is to be My Church, and named after My Name, must be in the pattern which I shall designate. Behold, I say unto you that when mine Apostles were upon the earth, even mine Apostles of olden time, behold, I ordained even twelve at the time of My ministry, and behold, ye know of a surety that I ordained twelve in Jerusalem, and from these twelve I ordained three to be the Presidency of My Church, even mine apostles Peter, James, and John, for they held the keys of Presidency, and to those things pertaining to the up-building of My Church. And ye would have this record had not those wicked ones removed this knowledge from these records which ye have, nevertheless there is sufficient written for ye to understand. Nevertheless these three which I chose, holding the office of Presidency remained part of the Twelve, for there was not a necessity that they should be separate at that time, yea, and after My resurrection ye have record and bear record that I visited the saints who were separated from those in Jerusalem, yea, even those who remained here upon this continent, and from those who were faithful I chose even twelve, and these I ordained to be Apostles to My Church, to govern the affairs of My Church in this part of My Kingdom for there were even two Quorums of Twelve in separate parts of My vineyard having authority and set up to govern that particular part of My Kingdom, and behold this is the pattern which I have set which is after the most Holy Order of God.

Nevertheless when I set up My Church by the hand of My prophet Joseph Smith, I separated the Presidency separate

48

from the Quorum of Twelve Apostles preparatory to that which was to follow. Behold it was not expedient to reveal further to My prophet Joseph Smith at that time, for I reveal line upon line, precept upon precept, for the benefit of My saints as the need arises, nevertheless I set this up preparatory to that which was to follow. Behold, I say unto you that it is expedient that ye ordain under My hand a Quorum of Twelve Apostles for not more than one hundred and forty-four stakes of My Church, over which they are to preside and govern, and be traveling High Priests bearing especial witness to Me and governing and setting in order all things pertaining to My work in that section of My Kingdom wherewith they are to preside, and thus likewise ye shall divide it according as the Spirit whispereth, and there shall be no disputations among you, and ye shall ordain Quorums of Twelve Apostles as need arises, and each shall be responsible to Me for their stewardship in that section of My Kingdom wherewith they shall govern, and ye shall put out of My sight these abominations ye have set up, which are like unto the abominations set up by that Great and Abominable Church which shall shortly receive the wrath of mine indignation.

Behold, ye also distort other principles of My Gospel, for ye have not understood and have not heeded those things which are most plain and precious which are contained in My Book, the Doctrine and Covenants, and ye have listed to that evil one which seeks to place himself at the head of My Church, for he hath crept into many of those who preside over the Church and by this means he hopeth to overthrow My Kingdom by bringing confusion into it, and by bringing compulsion upon My people, for he inspireth the minds and thoughts of man with great works, and they appeareth of great worth at the time, but afterwards bringeth only confusion and a stumbling block for My people, and by his many subtile means he gaineth control, but behold, I say unto you he shall be exposed, and be overthrown, and cast out, and at My coming, by My presence, be cast into outer darkness for the space of a thousand years and after that he shall be loosed for a little season to gather those that are his, and then shall the end come.

And again pertaining to the abominations ye have brought into My Church, behold, ye have placed the responsibility of the welfare of My Church upon the elders of My Church. Behold, I say unto you, this is an abomination unto Me, for at no time have I stated in My Book, the Doctrine and Covenants that the Elders preside over the welfare of My Church, for I have stated plainly that this responsibility remaineth in the Bishop and his councillors, for he presideth over the Aaronic Priesthood, and hath the complete responsibility in this matter. Neither hath he responsibility pertaining to the spiritual things of this Church, and if any hath a matter pertaining to a spiritual thing he must needs go to the head of his quorum or whichever be in charge and ask him, for I have not given to the Bishop of My Church this charge, but in temporal matters he hath charge and this is his calling. For it is not the calling of the Elders to be in charge over the welfare of My Church, but it is meet for them to be standing elders living My commandments, and exhorting the people to righteousness and expounding the scriptures in all humility, and assisting the Bishop in all things pertaining to temporal matters as requested and needed for the welfare of My Church.

And ye have said and written even that the Bishop is the Presiding High Priest, and therefore able to govern the quorums and instruct them in his ward. Behold, I say unto you, this is also an abomination unto Me, for a Bishop hath no authority over the Melchizadek Priesthood, and cannot calleth them to order or have any degree of authority over this Priesthood, but hath authority only as I have before mentioned. And behold, ye have begun to do even that which was of old, for they did this thing and from this came the most Abominable Church,

50

yea, even the Mother of Harlots and Abominations of the earth. For ye do not understand and comprehend the order of Heaven, and seek to establish your own order, which order was placed there by that most cunning one.

Neither can a Bishop preside over an Elder, nor a Seventy, nor a High Priest, but hath authority and can preside over a Quorum of Priests, nevertheless he may be a judge over each member of his Ward pertaining to temporal things, for he is appointed unto this having a knowledge of this by the Spirit of Truth.

Now this ye have read is most plain and easy to understand, and if there be any disputation concerning this matter ye are in error having not the Spirit, for those who do not have My Spirit cannot understand these things, for that which is carnal hath no understanding of those things pertaining to God, but things pertaining to the world and behold the wicked rage when they hear that which is the truth, for their hearts have been taken over by that evil one and they list to his desires, and plainness is contrary to their natures, and they seek after mysteries, but not qualifying themselves for this knowledge, behold, I say unto you, it destroyeth them, for are they not thieves? Behold, ye cannot come unto My Kingdom any other way but must enter at the straight gate living My laws and My commandments.

Behold, I say unto you that the Presidency shall preside over the several Quorums of Apostles as they are organized, and have the keys to preside even over one or more Quorums of Apostles, for thus is the order of My Church, yea, even patterned after the order of Heaven, and the President presideth over the whole Church, and is to be like unto Moses, yea, to be a seer, a revelator, a translator, and a prophet, having all the gifts of God which He bestows upon the head of the Church. But woe unto those in the Presidency of My Church who keep not and sustain not My commandments, for unless they keep

51

My commandments they have not the power, for not even the President of My Church hath this power if he keep not the commandment pertaining to these gifts, for wherein can ye receive a blessing from My hand unless ye keep the commandment pertaining to that blessing? Yea, woe unto those in the presidency of My Church who refuse My Word and live not My commandments, for did not I remove even Saul from his place when he rebelled against Me, for that which I have spoken shall surely come to pass and shall surely be enacted, for they shall be smitten and their abominations exposed. What then can ye say, for it is written and decreed that I will send one to set in order My Church, and that one appointed shall surely be smitten, for he putteth forth his hand and seeketh to steady the ark or God. He who hath an ear let him hear and he who hath an eye let him see. Behold, I say unto you, only by the Spirit of God can ye understand the things of God. Enter ye in at the straight gate and be saved, even at My coming, even the living and the dead, even so, Amen.

Section 19

Revelation received Jan., 1965

Behold, and give ear and hear the voice of your Savior, yea, even the still small voice that maketh tremble at every joint, yea hear your Savior who speaketh to you, even through a prophet chosen by Me. For I choose not after the ways of men, but choose those that men cast out and esteem as naught, for this is according to the prophecies that have been made.

Behold, I have sent My servant and there are those who have condemned him for receiving My Word and there are those that say he receiveth these revelations from Satan. Beware, those who disregard these words, for they shall be accountable before Me at that day. Behold, I say unto you that ye shall read them, and when ye read them, if ye find anything among them that teacheth that which is unrighteous, then ye shall know that they are false, but ye shall not find such among them, for they teacheth righteousness and cry repentance unto this people. Behold, again, I say unto you, and the still small voice pierceth to the centre, for it bringeth to light that which was hidden and searcheth the hearts of all men, yea, it commandeth the greatest among you, yea, if he who is the greatest among you shall with his wisdom prepare even a revelation like unto the least of these I have given to My servant whom I have called, then ye are justified in saying that ye are not sure that they are true. Nevertheless ye know that they are true, for that which teacheth righteousness cometh from above. And if the wisest among you are unable to write even as the least of these, then ye are under condemnation, for ye are like unto those who seeketh after a sign, for an evil and adulterous and an unbelieving generation seeketh after a sign. Behold, I say unto you I have chosen My servant, and in him I have placed My Spirit, and I speak to him even as I spoke to My servant Joseph Smith, for I did impress upon his mind those things that were expedient to the upbuilding of My Church, and he wrote them as I commanded. Nevertheless I appeared unto him and manifested Myself unto him in many ways, for great was his faith. And in no wise did he sin for he repented of his sins and he kept My commandments and was faithful even unto the end, and I have taken him unto Myself, and he spilled his blood upon the floor of the Carthage jail as a testimony against the wicked, yea, and they have suffered and have been smitten, and cursed with a sore curse even unto this day.

What say ye then if ye rebel against Me, and heed not the words of My servant? What then are ye likened unto? Yea, ye are likened unto salt that has lost its savor, and are good for nothing but to be trampled under foot, for My Spirit shall withdraw from you and ye shall be cast down from that where ye now stand. Yea, and all that is written concerning this matter shall surely come to pass even every whit. For I lie not, neither does My path vary even one iota.

Repent therefore, and begin to keep My commandments for I will not suffer you to mock My Word. Even so, Amen, and Amen.

Section 20

Revelation received May 30, and June 4th, 1965

Behold, I say unto you, Joseph Smith asked concerning which Church he should join, and in accordance with his desire and faith he received revelation restoring the knowledge of the Godhead to the earth. Behold, I say unto you, at this time I have again sent My servant for the purpose of rectifying many errors which have crept into My Church, the only Church upon the face of the earth in which lies the Priesthood. These errors, so as in times past, have come about through the efforts of wicked men who have been inspired not of Me, but by that evil one whose only desire is to destroy all that is good. I have given My servant revelations which are plain and clear, that bring to light those errors, and which also contain many important doctrines which are necessary for the upbuilding of My Church in these the latter days. Behold, I say unto you, if the leaders of this Church heed not these revelations they shall be cast off even to their ultimate destruction, but if the leaders of My Church heed the words of the prophets they shall again have the power of revelation which they have surely lost because of their failure to keep My commandments in the which I promised that if they kept not these commandments they would be damned. And surely I have kept My promise, for My Word cannot be stayed neither can it be turned aside, for it is just and true.

Purify yourselves, therefore, brethren, for the responsibilities yet to come. Cast off all unrighteousness among you, yea even cast off your selfishness, your strivings, and your quarreling, yea, even also your filthy thoughts, and place on your shoulders the armor of righteousness and of good works, for behold I come quickly.

Section 21

Revelation received June 3, 1965

Yea, and again, those that love Me shall keep My commandments I have given through My holy prophet and those who keep not My commandments and heed not My holy prophets shall be cut off from among My people that they may become a hiss and a byword, for there are some among those who claim to be leaders of My Church who are in league with that evil one and seek to overthrow My Kingdom, but they shall be exposed, and their sins shall be laid bare and those that come shall surely do it, for their wickedness is above all types of wickedness, for they seek glory for their own sakes as Satan did before the world was, and because of their wickedness they become like unto the Pharisees and hypocrites, and they stone and mock those that are sent because they are not like them and do not accept their carnal ways. Woe unto them, for their suffering shall be exquisite and wonderful, and only those that are worthy of this punishment can understand.

Behold, I say unto you, the time has now come that ye shall go forth and proclaim these revelations upon the housetop, yea, even by printing and even by teaching and if it so be that ye shall obtain disciples ye shall reveal all that ye have learned unto them, and if ye shall obtain opposition ye shall bear it patiently and murmur not for this is My testing. Fear not to go forth and proclaim this even unto all those who will listen, for I have commanded this and My Spirit shall be with thee to protect thee in all things that thou art prepared to do to the bringing forth of much righteousness unto this and future generations, for My Spirit shall overcome all, for the end draweth nigh, yea, and is even at the doors. Even so, Amen.

Section 22

Revelation Received September 15, 1968
Concerning the Nature of God
and the Creation of the World.

Behold, I say unto you, inasmuch as ye have asked Me in faith concerning God and the creation, and inasmuch as ye are confused by the doctrines of men, and their understanding of the creation, behold I will reveal unto you some of the truth ye have desired. For thou hast desired it in great faith and the teachings of men doth bother thee and ye can see where they do err.

Behold, I say unto you, I am Jehovah, and through my lineage comes the Saviors of worlds, and they are My only Begotten Sons, nevertheless, I have many sons, for there are many worlds. Behold, I say unto you, I am the Creator, for all worlds which are created are created through the power which I hold, and there is not anything that is created that is not created by that power. Behold, I say unto you, Jesus Christ, who walked upon this earth, is in the express image of my person, for he is My Son, for are not sons like unto their fathers? Because he was faithful in all things prior to his birth he was to be the only begotten of the father in the flesh. Now some have said that Adam is his father. Behold, I say unto you how could Adam be the Father of Jesus Christ, for Adam had many

59

sons and daughters of Eve and Jesus Christ could not then be his only begotten. Therefore they are in error, not having the spirit.

Behold, this knowledge is necessary for the salvation of man, for how can man worship someone whom he knoweth not?

Behold, I say unto you concerning Adam, is he not Michael the Archangel, yea even the father of all spirits? Was this not the fulfillment of the convenant? Yea, he did qualify himself to become as a God and through his righteousness did obtain salvation and did he not obtain many wives? And he did dwell upon an earth and did die according to all flesh, and because of his righteousness was exalted, and all that he obtained through righteousness became his forever and ever worlds without end, yea, even all his wives and possessions and his glory are from everlasting to everlasting. And because he was faithful he received the promise that his seed would be without number even as the stars of heaven are without number. And the promise was fulfilled, for God's promises will surely be fulfilled, yea, every whit, and he became the father of a numerous host of spirits, yea, and his firstborn having the right, became the Savior of the world, yea, even Jesus Christ the Redeemer, for that is the right of the First born in the spirit, to be a Redeemer for his brethren, even becoming their Father and God, and coming in the meridian of time to save them from their sins, then becoming the Son of God even Jehovah. For he then has all rights, powers, and privileges pertaining to this earth that His Father even Jehovah had on his earth and thus, through this Priesthood having neither beginning of days nor end of years, becomes the creator of worlds even for those who are righteous and are true and faithful upon this earth. Therefore he is both Father and Son. Whoso hath an ear let him hear and whoso hath an eye let him see, for none receiveth this knowledge but by the spirit, and I revealed this unto Joseph for he did have this knowledge and all the holy prophets from the begining, and the people received not the truth and listed to fables rather than truth, and therefore are cast off.

Behold, I say unto you, that man Adam is your Father and God and the only one with whom ye have to do, for is he not the father of your spirit, and also the progenitor of your earthly body? For he was true and faithful, and became a God, and under My direction even the direction of the Priesthood, even Jehovah, was placed upon this earth and did bring to this earth all the good things that did exist in his sphere, and planted a garden even a garden of glorious beauty. And he was commanded to take of the children of men a wife, and he called her name Eve, for she was the mother of all living, and thus he did mingle his seed with the children of this earth, and thus did all his creation, and thus did the generation of man begin. Because he did mingle his seed, he became as of the earth and subject to death, for did he not die so that his offspring of the spirit world could take unto themselves bodies so that they could become exalted through faithfulness like unto himself, for this is the law. Adam died that man might be, and men are that they might have joy. This same Eve was with Adam from the beginning and was one of his wives, and she did listen first to that cunning one and did mingle her seed with the seed of this earth first, and she did partake of that which was forbidden and became as mortal, and Adam mingled his seed with hers also and became mortal also being again subject to death. Behold I say unto you, there is no other way, and by disobedience he lost all recollection of the former existence, for a time, but through faithfulness and baptism, received this knowledge as at first and prophesied of his seed unto the last generation, and he shall come to the valley of Adam Ondi Ammon to sit and judge his posterity and require everyone according to his stewardship.

Whoso hath an ear let him hear, and mock not, for swift

61

shall be your destruction. Behold, I am Alpha & Omega, the beginning and the end, the light and life of the world, and I sent mine only begotten, and ye received him not, neither did ye regard his word, for he cometh as a thief in the night to reign as King of Kings and Lord of Lords, and none shall stay his hand. Even I come quickly, even so, Amen.